Castle Under Siege!

Chicago, Illinois

Raintree

© 2006 Raintree
Published by Raintree,
A division of Reed Elsevier, Inc.
Chicago, Illinois

Customer Service   888–363–4266

Visit our website at www.heinemannraintree.com

Printed and bound in the United States by Lake Book
Manufacturing, Inc.

10 09 08 07 06
10 9 8 7 6 5 4 3 2 1

**Library of Congress Cataloging-in-
Publication Data**
Solway, Andrew.
   Castle under siege!: simple machines / Andrew
Solway.
        p. cm.
   Includes index.
   ISBN 1-4109-1918-8 (library binding) -- ISBN 1-
4109-1949-8 (pbk.)
   1. Simple machines--Juvenile literature.   I. Title.

TJ147.S66 2005
621.8--dc22
                                    2005014549

Acknowledgments
The author and publishers are grateful to the
following for permission to reproduce copyright
material: AKG Images pp. 15 (left), 28 (top), 29
(bottom); Alamy p. 24 (Pixoi Ltd); Ancient Art &
Architecture p. 27; Beatriz and Kurt Dillard p. 12;
Bridgeman Art Library p. 23 (Pieter Brueghel/
Kunsthistorisches Museuem); Collections p. 20
(Michael Jenner); Corbis pp. 5 (Royalty-free), 11
(Angelo Hornak), 29 (top) (Chris Hellier); DK Images
p. 15 (right); England's Medieval Festival p. 19
(Herstmonceux Castle); Rex p. 7 (Paul Cooper);
Robert Harding Picture Library p. 8–9.

Cover illustration by Darren Lingard.

Illustrations by Kamae Design.

The publishers would like to thank Nancy Harris
and Harold Pratt for their assistance in the
preparation of this book.

Every effort has been made to contact copyright
holders of any material reproduced in this book.
Any omissions will be rectified in subsequent
printings if notice is given to the publishers.

The paper used to print this book comes from
sustainable resources.

Contents

Some words are printed in bold, **like this**. You can find out what they mean on page 30. You can also look in the box at the bottom of the page where they first appear.

Every King Should Have One

About 700 or 800 years ago, castles were really important. This time is known as the Middle Ages. Every ruler in the Middle Ages had a castle. Some kings or queens had a lot of castles!

Castles were built to be safe from attack. A ruler could control all of the countryside around the castle. A castle was also the ruler's home. **Knights** lived there, too. The knights were trained to fight anyone who attacked the castle.

Life in a castle was hard work—unless you were the ruler. Most jobs had to be done by hand. **Simple machines** made some jobs easier. In this book, we will learn about simple machines. We will also look at how simple machines were used to build, attack, and protect castles.

Hard work!

Building a castle was hard work! Most jobs were done by hand. Many workers were needed. A castle could take ten years to build. It might need 2,500 workers.

knight   in history, an important man who was trained to fight
simple machine   tool used to push or pull something

▲ This castle was built in the Middle Ages. It could stand up to an attack by an army.

Building a Castle

Stonemasons were very important. They built the castle's huge stone walls and towers.

A stonemason's most useful tools were **wedges**. Wedges were triangle-shaped pieces of wood. They were thin at one end and wide at the other. Wedges were used to cut stone.

A wedge is a **simple machine**. It turns a downward push into an outward push.

When a wedge is ▼ pushed downward into a block of stone, it pushes very strongly outward.

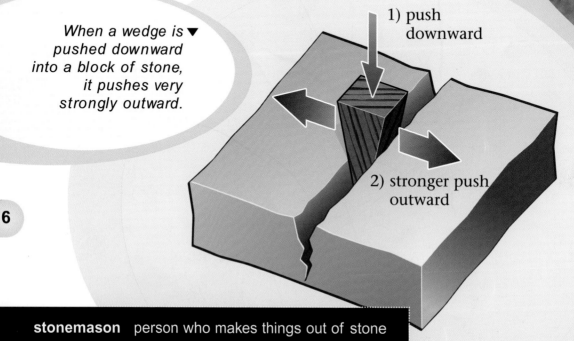

1) push downward

2) stronger push outward

stonemason	person who makes things out of stone
wedge	piece of wood or metal that is thin at one end and thick at the other

Stonemasons cut stone ▲
into blocks. They used a
hammer and chisel. A chisel
is a type of wedge.

Moving the stones

The cut stones had to be carried to the castle. They were usually carried in carts. The carts were pulled by horses.

Most castles were built on high ground. The sloping road going to the castle was a **simple machine**. The road was an **inclined plane**. An inclined plane has one end higher than the other. Lifting a heavy load is hard work. Moving a heavy load up an inclined plane is easier. However, a load has to travel farther when you use an inclined plane.

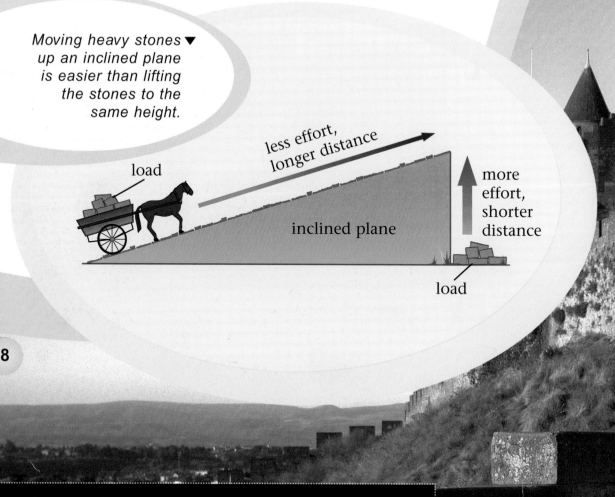

Moving heavy stones ▼ up an inclined plane is easier than lifting the stones to the same height.

less effort, longer distance

load

inclined plane

more effort, shorter distance

load

inclined plane flat surface that has one end higher than the other

▲ There is a path leading up to this castle. The path is a type of inclined plane.

Safe from Attack?

There were wars in the Middle Ages. Armies often tried to capture enemy castles. This was not easy! Soldiers would usually have to get up a steep hill. They would then have to get over a deep moat (lake). The castle's stone walls were too thick to be knocked down. The soldiers inside the castle could fire arrows at attackers.

One way to capture a castle was to surround it with an army. The army stopped people from going in or out. This was called a **siege**.

The people in the castle might run out of food. They might run out of water if the siege lasted a long time. However, castles could store enough food to last for months. Most castles also had a well, so they would not run out of water.

A castle is protected from▶ attack in many ways.

siege   when an army surrounds an enemy castle

Water protects castle on all sides.
Soldiers look out from high towers.
Thick walls are hard to get through.

Lifting the drawbridge

So, what actually happened in a **siege**? Usually the only way into a castle was the drawbridge. If the castle was attacked, the drawbridge was lifted. That way, no one could get in.

Most drawbridges worked using two long pieces of wood. These pieces of wood are **levers**. Levers are **simple machines**. Each lever was fixed at a point called the **fulcrum**. The levers moved around the fulcrum.

Soldiers pulled down on one end of the lever. The other end went up. This lifted the drawbridge.

▼ *The drawbridge was a narrow wooden bridge over the castle moat (lake).*

How a drawbridge works

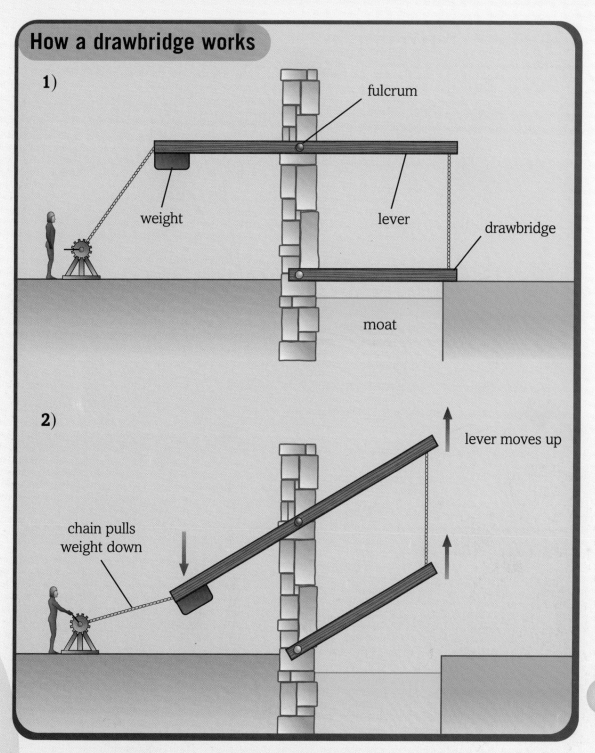

1)

fulcrum

weight

lever

drawbridge

moat

2)

lever moves up

chain pulls
weight down

fulcrum   fixed point that a lever moves around

lever   beam of some kind that can move around
a single point called the fulcrum

Under Siege!

In a **siege**, the attackers surrounded the castle. Yet they didn't get too close. The castle soldiers had crossbows!

Crossbows were deadly weapons. This was because a crossbow was very stiff. It was so stiff that an **archer** could not pull the string back with his hands.

The archer turned a handle to pull back the string. The handle turned a **screw**. A screw is a rod of metal with a spiral cut into it. The string was pulled back when the archer turned the handle. The string wrapped around the screw. The string moves more slowly than if it were pulled in a straight line. However, the pull is much stronger.

Make a screw!

*A screw is a rod with an **inclined plane** rolled around it. You can make a screw with a pencil and some paper. Cut a triangle shape out of paper. Starting at the wide end, roll the triangle around a pencil. This is a screw!*

pencil

paper triangle

archer   soldier who uses a bow to fire arrows
screw   rod of wood or metal with a spiral shape around it

screw

▼A crossbow from the Middle Ages.

arrow

handle

This is a different type of ▶ crossbow. The archer is turning the handle to tighten the string.

Siege towers had wheels ▼
and axles. This meant
they could be moved
close to castle walls.

axle

wheel

16

Siege towers

At the start of a **siege**, the surrounding army would often attack the castle. This was to find out if the castle was well protected. One way to attack was to use siege towers. These were tall, wooden towers on wheels.

The attackers pushed the siege towers up to the castle walls. Groups of soldiers stood at the top of each tower. The soldiers then jumped onto the castle walls.

The wheels on the siege tower made it easy to move. The wheels were joined to **axles**. An axle is a rod with a wheel at each end.

A wheel and an axle make a **simple machine**. It is much easier to move a heavy load on wheels than to drag it over the ground.

axle   bar with a wheel or wheels joined to it

Giant catapults

If the **siege** did not work, the attackers could try to break the castle walls. They used giant catapults to break the castle walls. Catapults could throw large stones at high speed.

A giant catapult used a **lever** to throw a stone. The lever was a long beam. It was fixed at a point called the **fulcrum**. On one end of the lever was a very heavy weight. On the other end was a strong band of material. This was called a sling.

Soldiers put a stone inside the sling. They used ropes to pull down the sling end of the lever. The lever was held down with a large pin. When the pin was pulled out, the heavy weight crashed down. This made the sling end of the lever fly up very quickly. The stone was thrown toward the castle.

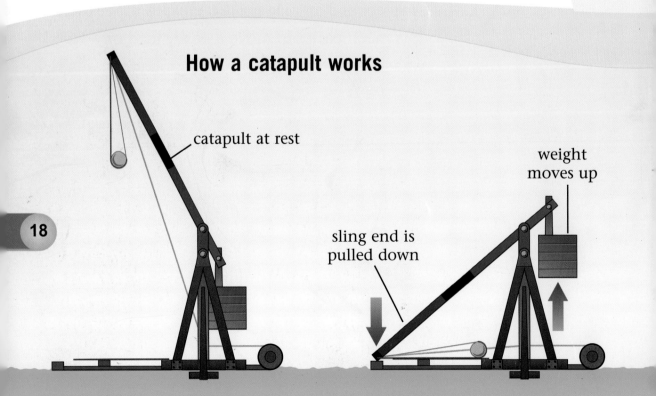

How a catapult works

catapult at rest

sling end is pulled down

weight moves up

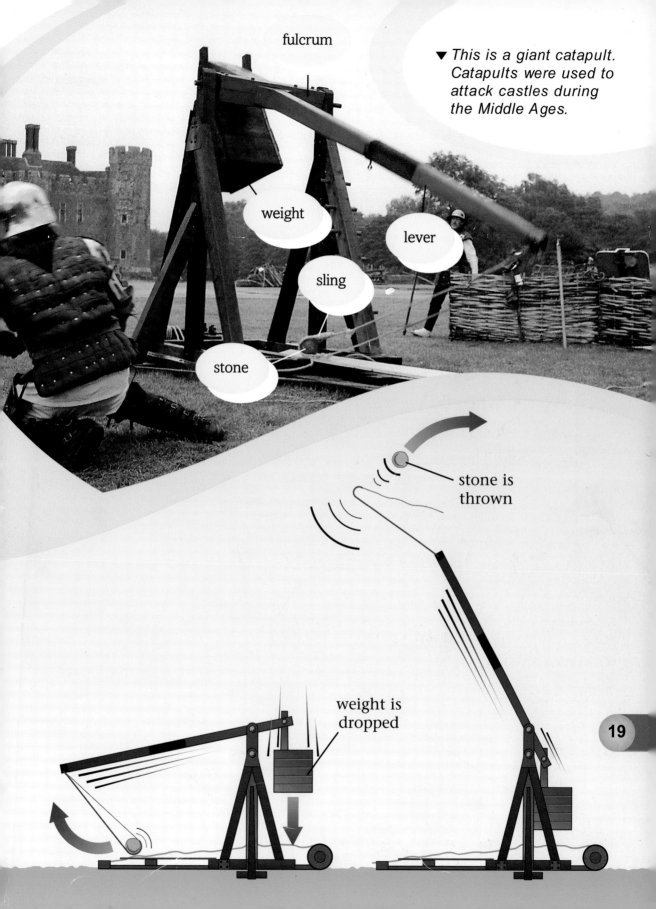

fulcrum

▼ *This is a giant catapult. Catapults were used to attack castles during the Middle Ages.*

weight

lever

sling

stone

stone is thrown

weight is dropped

19

▲ This castle wall has fallen down in the past. Stonemasons have tried to repair it.

Digging a tunnel

If the catapults did not work, the attackers could try to dig under the castle walls. The attackers dug a tunnel. They used the tunnel to make the castle wall fall down.

The diggers used shovels to dig out the soil. They used **levers** called crowbars to dig out big stones. Wooden posts held up the roof of the tunnel.

The tunnel was dug under the walls. The diggers then put dry wood around the wooden posts. Then, they set fire to the dry wood.

The posts holding the tunnel roof started to burn. The tunnel started to fall down. When this happened, the castle wall above the tunnel also fell down.

Crowbars

*Crowbars are levers. You press on the handle with a small push, or **force**. The force at the other end is much bigger. However, you have to move the handle a long way. The lifting end of the crowbar moves only a short distance.*

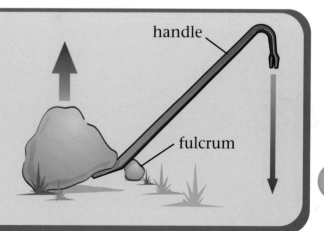

handle

fulcrum

force   push or pull

Clearing Up

What happened when the **siege** finished? No matter who won, the castle probably needed repairs. **Stonemasons** came to mend the walls. Some stonemasons used a crane to lift the heavy stone blocks.

The stonemasons' crane was powered by a huge wheel. This wheel was called a **treadmill**. Four people walked slowly around inside the wheel to turn it.

The crane used a wheel and **axle**. The treadmill was the wheel. The axle was a thick pole called the winding drum. The rope that lifted the stone wound onto the axle.

The wheel was much bigger than the axle. So, a small turning **force** on the wheel became a large force on the axle. However, the wheel had to move a long way to make the axle turn a small distance.

A stonemasons' crane ▶ was used in the Middle Ages to build large stone buildings.

treadmill   large wheel that people turn by walking inside it

axle

treadmill

▼ Pulleys are still an important part of cranes today.

pulley

Pulleys to help the pulling

The **treadmill** crane uses small wheels. The wheels help it lift heavy weights. These wheels are called **pulleys**.

A rope threads through the two pulley wheels. One wheel is joined to the crane. The other wheel is joined to the weight. The rope has to move twice as far as it would without the pulleys. This means the stone is lifted more slowly. However, the pull on the rope is only half as much as it would be without the pulleys.

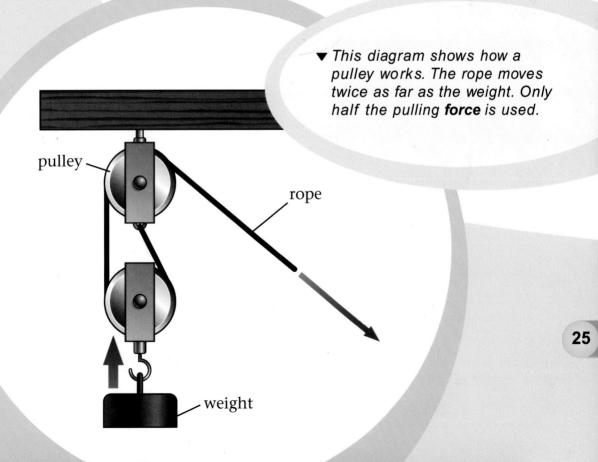

▼ *This diagram shows how a pulley works. The rope moves twice as far as the weight. Only half the pulling* **force** *is used.*

pulley

rope

weight

pulley   small wheel threaded onto a rope or chain to help lift heavy weights

Built for defense

Castles were the biggest and strongest buildings in the Middle Ages. It took a long time to build a castle. It needed a lot of workers. Most work was done by hand. However, the workers had **simple machines** to help them. They used wedges and inclined planes, for example.

A well-built castle was hard for an army to attack. Armies often had to use machines such as **siege** towers and giant catapults. Sometimes even these weapons were not enough. One answer was to wait for the people inside to run out of food and water.

Castles became easier to attack when a gun called the cannon was invented. Cannonballs could break down even the thickest stone walls. But that's another story!

Simple Machines

Wedges, inclined planes, screws, levers, wheels and axles, and pulleys are all simple machines. They can be used to make some kinds of work easier.

Wedges

This tool uses a type of wedge. Wedges push things apart strongly when you press down. This tool is used to chop wood.

Pulleys

Pulleys are small wheels with a rope threaded through them. With two pulleys, you can lift twice as much weight with the same effort. However, the rope has to be pulled twice as far.

Wheels and axles

A **siege** tower and a **stonemason's** crane have wheels and axles. Moving a load on wheels is easier than dragging it.

Inclined planes

An inclined plane is a slope. Pulling a heavy load up this is easier than lifting it straight up. However, the load has to move farther.

Levers

The drawbridge, the catapult, and the crowbar are all types of lever. A lever is a stiff bar or stick. It moves around a fixed point. This point is called the **fulcrum**.

Screws

A screw is like an inclined plane wound in a spiral. A crossbow uses a screw to pull back the string. With the screw, the archer can pull the string with much more **force**. However, winding the string back takes much longer than just pulling it.

Glossary

archer soldier who uses a bow to fire arrows. Archers were very important before the invention of gunpowder.

axle bar with a wheel or wheels joined to it. Often there are two wheels joined to an axle, one at each end.

force push or pull. You need a force to get something moving or to make something happen.

fulcrum fixed point that a lever moves around. It is sometimes called a pivot.

inclined plane flat surface that has one end higher than the other. Inclined planes help us move things up or down.

knight in history, an important man who was trained to fight. Many knights lived in castles.

lever beam of some kind that can move around a single point called the fulcrum. Levers can be used to raise a castle drawbridge.

pulley small wheel threaded onto a rope or chain to help lift heavy weights. Most cranes use pulleys.

screw rod of wood or metal with a spiral shape around it. Screws are often used to fix things together.

siege when an army surrounds an enemy castle. The army stops food from getting to the people in the castle.

simple machine tool used to push or pull something. Many simple machines were used during the Middle Ages to build castles.

stonemason person who makes things out of stone. Stonemasons used wedges to cut stones.

treadmill large wheel that people turn by walking inside it. In the past, treadmills were used to power some machines.

wedge piece of wood or metal that is thin at one end and thick at the other. The cutting edges on knives, axes, and other tools are wedge-shaped.

Want to Know More?

Books

- Royston, Angela. *Levers.* Chicago: Heinemann Library, 2001.

- Royston, Angela. *Pulleys and Gears.* Chicago: Heinemann Library, 2001.

- Royston, Angela. *Wheels and Cranks.* Chicago: Heinemann Library, 2001.

Websites

- http://www.cosi.org/onlineExhibits/ simpMach/sm1.html

Do you want to learn more about the different types of simple machines and how they work? Check out this exciting website to find out more and to try some interesting activities!

Find out about some crazy machines in **Wackiest Machines Ever!**

All machines rely on forces to make them work. Find out about forces in extreme sports in **The Extreme Zone**.

Index